HUMOROUS POEMS
EXASPERATED PARENTS
AND
MISUNDERSTOOD CHILDREN

WRITTEN BY

MICHAEL . J . MORTON

ILLUSTRATED BY

CHRISTINA MORTON

TREBONNIE STUDIOS PUBLISHING

CONTENTS

Trebonnie Studios

Published by Trebonnie Studios Publishing, November 2008.

THE FAMILIES

The Bossy-Boots

Mum is called Millicent (Millie for short). She works as a school cook and is a terrible gossip and chatterbox. She has a good sense of humour and is a pushover for the children.

Dad is called Royston (Roy for short) and is a driving instructor .He is opinionated and thinks he is always right. He is very direct and does not suffer fools gladly.

Jerome is aged 12. He is easily led by his peers and has some objectionable habits. He is not academic but quite a sporty and likeable lad.

Melissa is aged 10. She is being taught to play the piano by the long-suffering Mr Mould. She is bright but, like her father, opinionated and always right (according to her). She is very vain and a bit of a goody two shoes.

Jasmine is aged 8 and a spoilt, naughty and noisy brat. She bullies at school, is rude, unruly and jealous of any competition from whatever quarter.

Marmalade is the family pet cat. He is as unruly as the children and likes his own way.

The Smarty-Pants

Mum is called Daphne and doesn't go out to work. She nags both husband and children and rules the roost. She tries to be prim and proper but is a bit of a snob. She likes ready meals, house and home magazines and coffee mornings. She has a lady in to help with the housework.

Dad is called Giles and works as a Tax Inspector. He is a bit insufferable, does a lot of overtime and always visits the pub for a drink after work. He is on a short fuse for most of the time.

Timothy is aged 11 and quite obnoxious. He is a highly intelligent know-all and doesn't let anyone forget it. He can be a loner and a bookworm. Not very good at sport although will give it a try.

Tabitha is aged 9. She is a girly girl, often in her own dream world. Dressing up and dancing are her favourite activities along with her doll collection. She is imaginative and admires her mother.

Tristrum is aged 4 and always getting into scrapes. He is over inquisitive, annoying in his habits and ways and is constantly asking unanswerable questions.

Tansy is aged 3 Months. She is a little doll.

COOKING

'I baked a cake last yesterday, my mummy helped a bit.
She got things from the cupboard and made the cooker lit.'

'It's mainly made of white stuff, with eggs and sugar too,
Then once I mixed in fruit and nuts it felt like stirring glue.'

'A little bit fell on the floor when mummy was upstairs.
So I scraped it up and put it back. There wasn't many hairs.'

'My hands got very dirty when I had to clean my shoe.
Cos all the heel and instep got stuck up with doggy poo.'

'My mummy said I should have washed my hands again. I'd
say That's probably the reason why the cake is very grey.'

It's a cake for daddy's birthday. I learnt to cook at school.
Dad said it tasted lovely, so I made him eat it all.

'Poor daddy wasn't well today, he had a fearful tummy.
I felt all right, it must have been the food he had from mummy.

Thoughts of Jasmine

Making cakes is really exciting. Mummy lets me stand on a chair and mix all the stuff in a bowl but the sticky goo on my hands seems to get everywhere. Mummy told me off for playing outside and not washing my hands but I couldn't reach the sink. The bits of dirt soon disappeared into the mixture so I didn't need to tell mummy about it. When it was cooked I took it to daddy and watched him eat it all up. The doctor said daddy had been made ill by some food, but we never found out what it was.

Mummy's Thoughts

Jasmine really wanted to cook something for daddy's birthday and, silly me, I thought a cake would cause the least trouble. It has taken me two hours to clean up the worst of the mess and I'm still finding sticky bits on the floor and cupboard doors. I only popped upstairs for a minute or two but she still had enough time to play with the dog, dig in the garden and then put her dirty hands back into the mixing bowl. I tried to throw it all away but she watched me like a hawk. I didn't have the heart to stop her giving it to daddy and he, stupid idiot, ate it. I'm not surprised he was sick. Serves him right for being so greedy.

PIANO LESSONS

I'm learning the piano and my teacher says I try,
In fact I show such promise that my efforts make him cry.
He told me he wears earplugs to cut out other noise
So he'll only hear my music, which is what he most enjoys.

My mother thinks Plaisir D'amour is what I play the best,
So I play and play and play it while she goes to have a rest.
It must be so relaxing cause when I go to peep,
Her head's beneath her pillow and she's almost fast asleep.

My dad said he would listen but he's very very busy,
As my hands flow fast along the keys it almost makes me dizzy.
He's lots and lots of work and though he seems to be quite ill
He cannot seem to work without his noisy hammer drill.

My brother was at home today but when he heard me play
He said the local farmer needed help to cut his hay.
We live in Oxford Circus so I really wonder how
The farmer has a field of grass and where he keeps his cow.

My time is up. I've closed the lid and finished for today.
I'll change into my tennis gear and go outside to play.
My teacher, who is thirty but looks more like eighty-eight,
Always gallops down our drive before he vaults our garden gate.

Melissa's Thoughts

I don't practice the piano every day but all the family let me have the whole room to myself when I do. The foot pedals are a bit difficult to reach but I can jump up and down on them when the music says play loud. Some of the notes are difficult and I don't always play the right ones but it always seems to sound OK. Mummy and Daddy don't listen very often as they are very busy. My teacher must be very old and has to visit the toilet lots of times, but he still keeps fit by running after every lesson.

Mummy's thoughts

How can someone so small make such a terrible noise? Poor old Mr Mould must be tearing his hair out. I'm sure Melissa must play the occasional right note but you can't distinguish them from amongst all the wrong ones. Thank goodness for the washing machine and vacuum cleaner. It's all right for dad, he can disappear off into his shed, lucky devil.

MY BEST FRIEND

My best friend is called Plonky
And he's very hard to spot.
I'm probably the only friend
That he has ever got.

He creeps around at dead of night
When no one else can see
And throws my toys around the floor
Then puts the blame on me.

At night time when I'm sleeping
With my arm around my Ted
He snuggles in beside me
And widdles in my bed.

At school when I'm not looking
He pulls Samantha's hair.
Puts paint inside her schoolbag
And glue upon her chair.

Why is it that he's naughty?
Whilst I'm so very good.
I can't really do without him
Though I sometimes wish I could.

Tristrum's Thoughts

I tidied my room like mummy said and then, when I was in the toilet, Plonky threw all my things on the floor. Mummy said she didn't believe me and that I must have done it but I didn't. Even at school I get the blame for things he does and teacher told me off for getting Samantha's dress all torn and sticky. tell Plonky not to get me into trouble but he just laughs and takes no notice. He is very much like me so I suppose it must be difficult to tell us apart.

Mummy's thoughts

If Tristrum thinks he can get away with his naughtiness by blaming it on his imaginary friend he's got another think coming. I had to give Samantha's mummy some money last week to have her dress cleaned and repaired. His teacher says he is disruptive and needs some discipline so his dad will have to take him in hand. I blame the teachers who should have more control. Don't we pay our taxes to have them teach our kids how to behave? Anyone would think it was our fault.

I WANT

'I want, I want, I want some,'
Said Jasmine Bossy-Boots.
'You bring me back a pound of sweets
And lots of juicy fruits.

'And don't forget that list of toys
I want my friends to see
That anything I want I get.
They'll really envy me.'

'If you don't bring me what I want
I'll shout and scream and fret.
I'll hold my breath and turn so blue
You'll have to call the vet.'

'I'll stamp my feet and smash your plates.
Set fire to the cat.
I'll saw the legs off all the chairs.
Now what d'you think of that.'

Because there were no sweets or toys
When mum came in from town.
Jasmine flew into a rage
And pulled the curtains down.

She held her breath and turned bright blue
Her mother stared aghast.
The doctor said. ' If you persist
Next time could be your last' .

Jasmine's Thoughts

I never get anything I want. All my friends have lots and lots but mum and dad are so mean. I hate them. If I hold my breath for a long time I faint and dad gives me things to make me feel better. I do lose my temper occasionally and sometimes accidentally break something. When I'm old enough and leave home I will be able to do anything I want and fill up my house with all my favourite things. I will have a lady in to do all my housework and sit and read and eat sweets all day long.

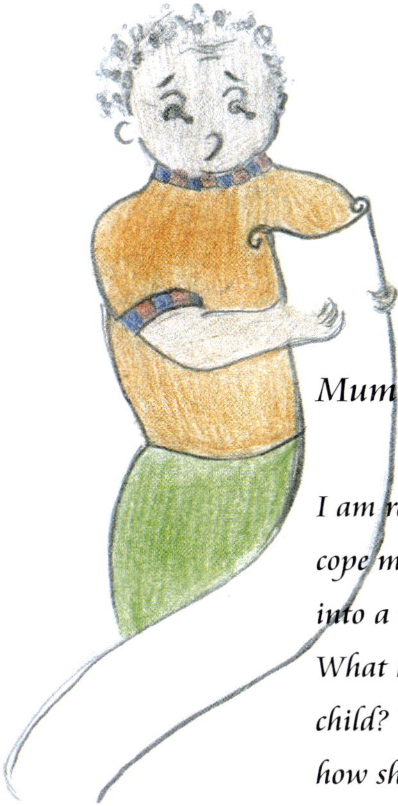

Mummy's thoughts

I am really at my wits end and don't feel I can cope much longer. She is never satisfied and flies into a violent rage when she can't get her way. What have we done to deserve such a troublesome child? We have given her everything and this is how she treats us. She smashes anything to hand when she is in one of her moods. I try to be firm but her father always gives in and lets her have what she wants. She is a spoilt brat who needs discipline.

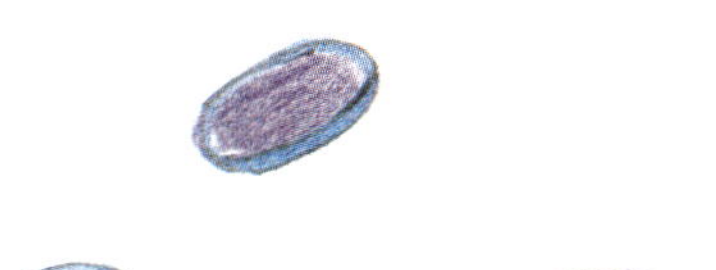

BOASTFULNESS

'I'm the brainiest boy in this country'
Said Tim, 'in fact if I probe,
'I'm sure it will be, plain for all folks to see,
I'm the brainiest boy on the globe'.

'My cerebral prowess is stunning
With a memory second to none,
My brain's a computer; I don't need a tutor,
There's nothing that I haven't done'.

'I was six when I got into Cambridge
And by seven secured my M A,
Then before reaching ten employed 52 men
With an income of ten grand a day'.

As he thought of his brilliance his head grew,
Like a beach ball attached to his face,
Then he floated away and was just heard to say,
'I'm the brainiest boy up in space'.

Timothy's Thoughts

My dad says that people with brains like mine are never any good at sport and I agree with him. I come top in everything academic I do and this makes my classmates jealous. They call me a four-eyed swot, but I don't care because they will be factory workers when I'm running my own business. I have not yet come across any one brainier than me and don't think I ever will. My ambition is to be emperor of the world.

Daddy's thoughts

He always was a bright child and could read at 6 months. We have spent a fortune sending him to all the best schools to give him the best possible start. Unfortunately this has turned him into an insufferable snob who thinks we are not good enough for him. He spends all his time with his nose in a book or on his computer. I just want a normal son to take to football matches and kick around with. One day, if he keeps on getting up peoples noses he will get his comeuppance.

FAIRIES

'Have you ever seen a fairy,' Melissa said to Nell.
'They live beneath the mushrooms, each has a silver bell.'

'I haven't seen them,' Nell replied,' but heard their tinkling bells,
Just over by that compost heap, the one that really smells.'

'That can't be so' Melissa said,' all fairies smell so sweet.
The bluebell patch is where they exercise their tiny feet.'

'Each fairy has a flower that it tends from break of day.
They do not get a moments rest or any kind of pay.'

'They do it cos they're fairies, and that's what fairies do.
When you become a fairy, well then you'll do it too.'

Melissa's Thoughts

I want the fairies to come into my garden and play but they never do. I've caught a glimpse of them sometimes when I am sitting in the garden with my eyes shut. If I am very very quiet I can hear their tiny silver bells. Nell hasn't seen them but I think she might have heard their bells. When I get older I might become a fairy and live in the woods. Daddy says fairies don't exist but mummy says men and boys are too noisy and frightening for fairies to show themselves.

Daddy's Thoughts

Melissa spends all day in a dream world. It's about time she got those silly notions of hers out of her head. Fairies indeed. It'll be dwarves and Pixies next. She should spend more time reading and doing her homework. The teachers don't seem to care what the kids do nowadays, not like when I was at school. Hankering after fairies won't get her a job.

SCHOOL

'My mummy says my teacher Mrs. Clark is very nice,
But everything I tell to her I have to say it twice.
I don't know if she's deaf or maybe isn't very bright,
Or praps she's got someone at home who keeps her up all night.'

'She's very tall and has a crimson pimple on her nose
And mummy says that somehow she has got some pigeon's toes.
I wonder where she got them and how the pigeon stands,
Or does he fly around all day and never ever lands.'

'Daddy thinks that teachers have a very easy life.
There's lots of holidays and stuff and never any strife.
I think he's right cos Mrs. Smith was absented last week.
I heard a teacher say she's off again with that same Sikh.'

'My best friend Simon Dimmock says his dad's
leg is a wood.
He might take me for a walk there if I'm very very good.
His leg must be ginormous and cover all our town.
I hope I'm not around when he decides to put it down.'

'My mum is very careful case I'm bitten by an At,
But lots of people wear them and I always worry that
They'll leap off heads and bite me till my arms and legs
are raw.
It isn't fair to be so cruel when I am only four.'

'When I get home from school I'll have to see my baby sister.
My mummy says her bottom is just one gigantic blister.
I don't know how she got it but it's very very smelly
And dad says I will get one too if I watch too much Telly.'

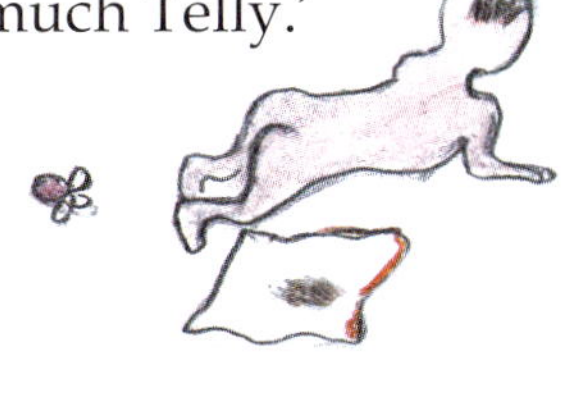

Tristrum's Thoughts

I like Mrs. Clark. The big spot on her nose moves when she talks. Does a spotty nose make you deaf? How does Simon's dad get into his house? Perhaps he goes in and leaves his leg behind as the garden. How do hats fly? I've never seen one with wings but they sometimes fly about in windy weather. My dad says that my teachers get lots of money and don't work much. I want to be a teacher when I grow up. I made a birthday card for my dad out of a toilet roll. My teacher said it was very good and very suitable. Daddy put it on the top shelf of our cupboard.

Teacher's Thoughts

Tristrum is a likeable boy but he will keep staring and shouting at me. He has some very strange ideas and during art classes draws hats with wings, men with big green legs and a host of other weird things. Still, having met his dad the other day at the open evening perhaps his odd ways are understandable. He thinks we are all idle layabouts and that the school should take upon itself his parental responsibility.

DISOBEDIENCE

'I'll just sit in the sun', Jasmine said to her mum,
Disregarding advice she should not,
But the tan that she got wasn't brown, it was red
And her skin grew incredibly hot.

Her temperature rose two degrees at a time,
Until at one hundred and nine,
Jasmine's back could be used to fry bacon and eggs,
Served with chips and a small twist of lime.

As the weather grew colder, the glow she gave off
Was sufficient to warm up her house.
By the end of the year she could heat the whole street
Just by waving a discarded blouse.

Soon her fame spread to Seeboard and then to Seagas,
Who fought for her frame without pity,
For the power emitted was now at a rate
To supply the demands of a city.

For the next year or two the intensity grew,
As she sat at the heart of the grid,
But the strength of her load caused the grid to explode.
Then darkness came down like a lid.

And so ends this sad tale, which happened because
She ignored the advice of her mum.
Incandescent and white, in the dead of the night,
They sent her to heat up the sun.

Jasmine's Thoughts

I want to have a tan like all those models on the telly. I thought that if I sat in the sun for an hour it would give me a nice olive skin and lots of people would ask me to model for them. Mum told me not to, but what does she know, she is always telling me what to do. Unfortunately I fell asleep for quite a long time and my skin was red and sore when I woke up. Mum and dad said they could feel the heat coming off my body and although it was cold we had to turn the heating off.

Mummy's Thoughts

I don't know how many times I've told her not to sit in the sun and to put sun cream on when she goes out. But does she listen? Of course not. I told her what would happen and now she is so sore and blistered that she can't lie down. The doctor tried to get her temperature down but it keeps on rising and I'm getting a bit worried. I really don't know where it will all end.

UNTIDINESS

'Your room is so untidy',
Said Tim's mum with a menacing scowl.
'There's so much on the floor, I can't open the door
To dig out the dirt with my trowel'.

'That heap of dirty washing,
Has pure methane at its core,
The festering pile will explode in a while
And blow out the windows and door'.

'Just stay in your room till you've cleared it,
I'll count to one thousand and ten.
Even dustmen would blench at the foul smelling stench
That's exuding from your den'.

Of course, Tim took no notice
And the pile of rubbish grew,
Till it filled all the space, right up to his face
And he turned a shade of blue.

Then the bugs fed on scraps and grew fatter.
They gobbled the rubbish as well.
Soon they all became big, one the size of a pig,
Tight around its fat neck hung a bell.

When they finally prised the door open,
There lay Tim on the floor, but no mess
And a hole in the wall, three feet wide, four feet tall,
What had made it they just couldn't guess.

Timothy's Thoughts

I can't see the point of tidying and cleaning. Everything soon gets messy and dirty again and needs re-doing. I've got better things to do with my time. As long as I can get into my bed and use my computer I don't care about the mess. Mummy moans about my dirty clothes but, as daddy says, it's a woman's job to wash them and put them away. I didn't ask to be born you know. I don't notice any smell but sometimes when I try to sleep I imagine that I can hear noises. Some of my things have disappeared and I think Tabitha or Tristrum must have taken them, although they deny it.

Mummy's Thoughts

I don't know what I am going to do about that boy. The smell in his room makes me feel sick but he doesn't seem to notice it. I will not be treated as his personal slave so his washing can stay there until he brings it out. I blame his father for setting a bad example but even he won't venture into Timothy's room. Tim complains that Tabitha and Tristrum take his things but I know it can't be true, as they won't go in his room either. The cat is always scratching at his door to get in, I can't imagine why.

MY HOLIDAY

'We went on holiday last week
Quite very very far.
We stayed inland at Duddy No
And daddy drove the car.'

'They put us in a gusset house
The beds were hard and lumpy.
The lady there was very nice
But the old man very grumpy.'

'My daddy said the old man
Had some wood upon his back.
I stared but couldn't see any
And he just stared right back.'

'The people there spoke funny
Whenever we were near.
But spoke just like the rest of us
When they thought we couldn't hear.'

'I heard it on the radio
We have to save the Wales.
But I've seen it, they won't get my help
It's full of rain and gales.'

Tristrum's Thoughts

I got very bored in the car when we went on Holiday and spent some of the time asleep. When we got there I wanted to go straight onto the beach but daddy said we had to put all our cases somewhere. We went to a big house and a man I didn't like said we could only have one room even though there were lots of empty ones. I couldn't understand what any of the people said so they must have all had bad colds brought on by the wet and windy weather. My teacher said that people who live in Wales are called Jonah, but most of them where we went were called Jones.

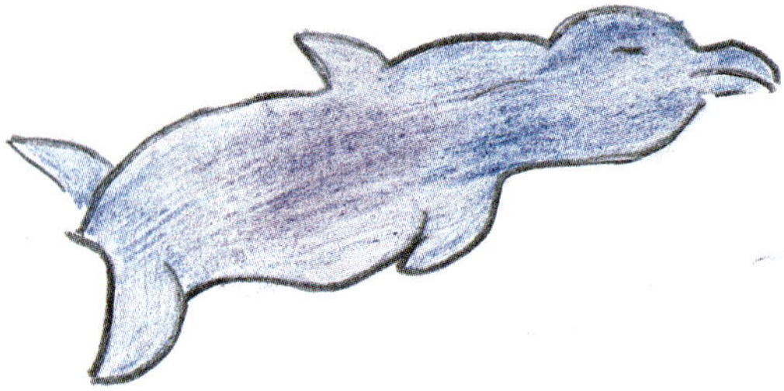

The Landlady's Thoughts

Since Hugh lost his job in the mines I've had to take in Bed and Breakfast holidaymakers to make ends meet. The English think they are so superior and their kids don't know how to behave. The little boy keeps staring at Hugh and sticking his tongue out. I don't know where they get the money for all these holidays, still we will take as much off them as we can. It's a good job they can't speak Welsh and hear what we are saying about them.

MARMALADE

We have a cat called Marmalade; he's ginger, tall and thin.
When we go out he caterwauls and all his friends come in.

They jump up on the furniture, then claw my Wilton rug.
When we get home he's all alone and looking rather smug.

In daylight hours he sleeps and eats, then makes the chairs his own,
But spends the whole night strutting, full of male testosterone.

He digs holes in the garden and then he fills them in.
Chews grass and eats the flowers, then scavenges the bin.

Sometimes when we're lucky he lets us stroke his fur
And if he really likes it he starts his motor purr.

We really like old Marmalade and I think he likes us.
We'll keep him here forever cause he isn't any fuss.

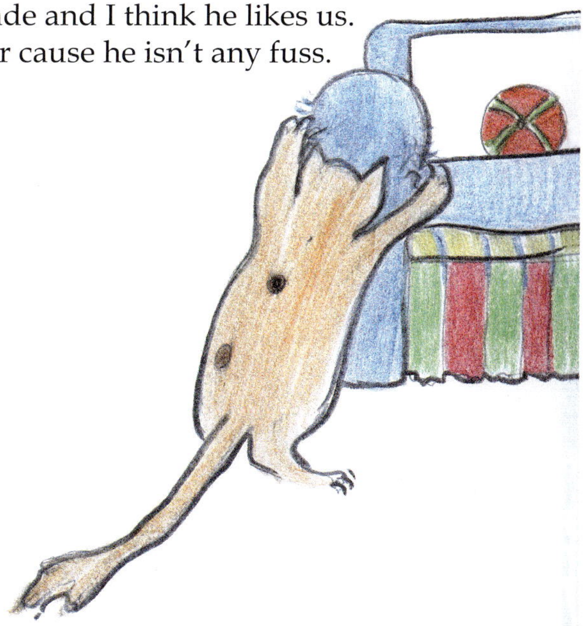

Marmalade's Thoughts

I quite like the big people but they won't let me just get on with my life. They chase off all my friends so I can only see them when the big people go out. I like to rest during the day, but quite often they disturb my sleep and don't put food down when I want it. I like the night-time because I can meet up with all my mates and go bird stalking. Sometimes they leave food in the bin and I have to knock it over and search through the contents to find it. This is very inconvenient as I get very dirty and have to wash.
In the evening when I'm cosy and snug it's quite nice to be stroked and petted but I soon let them know when I've had enough. I won't leave here because where else could I get warmth and meals for nothing.

Daddy's Thoughts

It's nice to have a family pet, but Marmalade really tries our patience. We put in a cat flap for him but he doesn't seem willing to stop other cats coming in. They make a mess everywhere and pull lumps out of our rugs. He's ruined my vegetable plot and dug up all my seedlings so now it looks like a moonscape. I couldn't sleep last night because of all the wailing and spitting outside our window and this morning I found the contents of our bin all over the lawn. But he is a real character so I wouldn't swap him and the kids love him to death.